Hiking the Rugged Shore

Hiking
— THE —
Rugged
Shore

CAROL LEAVITT ALTIERI

MADISON, CONNECTICUT
2019

Cover & Book Design by Words by Jen (Branford, CT)

ISBN 978-0-578-61403-8

Printed in the U.S.A.

DEDICATION

I put down these memorandums of my affections in honor
of tenderness, in honor of all of those who have
been conscripted into the brotherhood of loss...
— Martha Whitmore Hickman

For Frank Scot and Michael Altieri and Grandchildren:
Jacob, Alyssa, Lianna, Hannah, Michael, Jr.
Joseph, Mark, Mason and Isla

AND IN LOVING MEMORY:
Frank Anthony Altieri, April 11, 1932 - October 18, 2011
Alicia Ann Altieri, March 4,1962 - August 8, 2008

A DRINK OF WATER

by Seamus Heaney

She came every morning to draw water
Like an old bat staggering up the field;
The pump's whooping cough, the bucket's clatter
And slow diminuendo as it filled,
Announced her. I recall
Her grey apron, the pocked white enamel
Of the brimming bucket, and the treble
Creak of her voice like the pump's handle.
Nights when a full moon lifted past her gable
It fell back through the window and would lie
Into the water set out on the table.
Where I have dipped to drink again, to be
Faithful to the admonishment on her cup,
Remember the Giver fading off the lip.

TABLE OF CONTENTS

PART I

Lianna

"Comforter, where is your comforting? Mary mother of us,
Where is your relief?" — *Gerard Manley Hopkins #14*

The sky turns gold-orange and I celebrate Lianna
a gift cherished who redeems my shattered heart.
My granddaughter uplifts my poetic quest
and shields my soul.

During vacation, she loves to dive from high cliffs
and swim in the Atlantic and jog over miles
of rolling hills.

In our yard, with jean shorts and backpack,
she strains, pulls roots and weeds
that push up and assail the land.
Like a Japanese gardener raking perfect
rows of sand in a Zen Garden,
she cleans dead leaves
from the under covers to open up
the backyard view and pond.

I love the way she *unlocks my frozen sea.*
Immersed in tilling earth, seeding the garden,
she places her Norah Jones sounds
beside her as she sings.

The orchid of her face unfolds gracefully
and I glow with a slow flame
from her echoing reflection.

Wild Grace (Genetic Jeopardy)

I came from seashells, starfish and ocean flora.
Angel-struck from amniotic fluid,
commingled cells from England,
Canadian and French DNA.
Born before contraception.

Upthrust layers
of multicolored rock
encircled by rugged landlocked orchards.
In the nooks and crannies of my kingdom,
my curiosity multidimensional.

An artist and explorer,
with reservoirs of lustrous energy.
This body could ford a river
on wilderness treks.
And much later, consecrated
by Mediterranean droplets
of a baptismal river.

Limb by limb, branched
wanting to be everywhere.
Wrinkles flare underneath my eyes.
Knees hampered by repair
rock with hip-hop dancing legs.
Buds of orchids entangle
with alien plant life.

But oh, psychic demons unleash
dark forces. Face framed with shadow,
cathartic with tears; light of distant days
pours through white pines.

Farmer Roscoe (The Philosopher) ca 1937
Painting by Ivan Olinsky "suggests man's attitude toward life and the soil"

When the sun crosses the vernal equinox
the fields bleached by snow
convert to islands
of brown green, cradled by the hills.

Every morning, I take out the heavy-boned horses
to pull the plow next to a little valley
and turn up the squirming earthworms.
I dig weeds and turn up rich-smelling
spadefuls of soil.
I plant peas laying them out in rows
make grooves for cucumbers, squash,
carrots and lettuce.
Rabbits, woodchucks and raccoons steal
under the fences.
The sun warms deep into the earth
through branches of bare trees.
Sap begins to flow.

Birds migrate to feeding grounds:
meadows, woodlots, brooks and fields.
Warblers and hummers erupt from branches
and grace my farm with cascades
of twitters, trills and songs.
The winged gods of high places with eyes
like black pearls, glossy as midnight,
with fleeing silhouettes
scan for prey then vanish over the mountain.

Every night, after tilling, I tuck my work horses
in before I hand milk my cows
feel my bones blaze and skin effervesce.
This farm is in my heart and issues into my mind
and my fanned hands over everything.

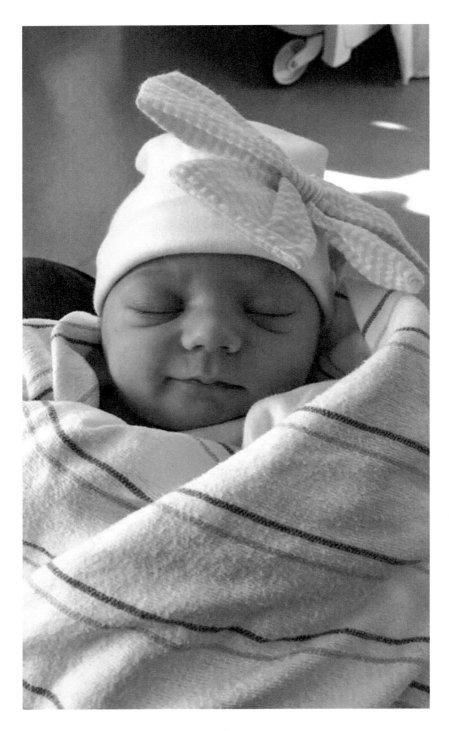

El Dorado

Holding my new baby girl, time stops.
I carry her down to the sand from a courtyard by the sea.
With thundering waves rolling in, we breathe
the invigorating air off the ocean.

Alicia, in a state of grace captures me
by her eyes, lifting her head to see
her mother. A soul, a heart, a rosy-pink body,
a tiny mouth with my skin
and father's blue eyes.

Perched in a shawl of nursing arms,
she is embraced by uneasy happiness,
a microcosm of all that is perfect
and vulnerable.
I hope to possess a secret amulet
that will protect her from life's monster traps.

We breathe together, I stare at her,
and see the sea reflected in her eyes
as she unfolds a morning's radiance
like the rare bird the Resplendent Quetzal.

She smiles in the sanctuary of my cradling
as I sing a roundelay of love.

Portrayal

Here's a painting of a woman I know.
She's sitting up in her bed reading,
All the Light We Cannot See.
In her night sky, gossamer rays unfold
in a shroud of mist as erratic as the wind.

She has survived
losses too heavy to lift.
She is growing older listening to spirits
and dreaming of the past family who sends messages.

She still feels her mother's voice saying
That is forbidden! With her it was always forbidden.
She's rather listen to her father who farmed
and planted fruit trees.

Her husband choreographed many adventures
and coaxed her to play. He extended
his Mediterranean light and a garden of flowers.
And shared in a kiss that has lasted this long.
Farewell my generous one, she says.

They created three children.
She saw the sea as a sacred source
and the moon move across the sky.

It Didn't Start With You*

I still walk the fields and earth
though as if a Cicada Killer
has paralyzed me.
I feel the confines of being buried alive.
The strain of a country cemetery
traps my intensity.

You never know what can happen.
The threads from the life Alicia shared
wraps to a kind of paralysis.
What sense can we make of our lives
after such an amputation?

I saw in her actions only playfulness
vibrancy and love. Without understanding,
I've read many times, *A Broken Heart Still Beats*.

I move in and out of shadows.
We met for the last time at the aquarium
during vacation in Cape May.
Captivated, we watched multi-colored
rainforest frogs.

The country landscape where Alicia is buried
abounds with Sweet Leaf Fern.
Virginia Creeper trembles and trails
over stone walls.
Seeds of grasses and wildflowers scatter.

I smell the falling leaves
as her son, father and I
sit on a granite bench.
Pines and oaks will safeguard her here.
We turn away, silent and solemn,
past old red barns
and unplanted fields.

Fracking Despair

Drilling down into Marcellus layers around the clock,

a cloud of polluted exhaust like a windstorm in his blood

invades elements of once beautiful pasture land.

Dust spreads over the sun of his mind

Acropolis of overturned earth, crack open the shale.

Layers of arms, legs and bones grieve. A gargantuan death

machine continues to dig a black hole

deep into the earth to shatter millions of cells, depopulating

flesh, desiccating lungs. Remaining energy releases viscerally

to trembling and shaking. Fear and anxiety leave him.

Strangled, the last breath quiets his chest.

Over his once strong shoulders, his pasture of wild flowers

scarred by blasting rock.

Inner Dresden

The mastered denial
the labored breathing, stopped.

The night he dies, the Chevy Truck's
headlights rise in the driveway.

He falls in the garage
on the cement floor.
His big blue eyes open strangely.
I give the kiss of breath,
try to pump his chest
and feel pale, cold skin.

Shrapnel cuts into my chest.

Much later, I will give away
the Henredon bed and bureau
and pack up all the bird sculptures
and paintings.
Roll up the oriental rugs he loved.

The nature sanctuary will sink
in to an elegy of ghosts
as memories of the Dresden
of inwardness seizes me.
I will shatter in a million pieces.

Silence of the Backyard Sanctuary

Night ran
her course, from heaven
layered and arranged.
Colonial house framed by trees planted:
Hawthorn, Dawn Redwood,
Mountain Ash, Dogwoods, Spruce,
Pines, Tulip, Birch in winter cloaks.
Hedgehogs, now comatose
that once scuttled out
of alleyways underground.
Brown ferns fuel over the garden.
Lichen cast shafts of sunlight.
Trespassers crush and crunch
acorns and pine cones.
Carrion Crows turn away
with sideways glance
and fly back into the woods.
Gathering of birds assemble,
settle on the feeder
seeking winter refuge.
A whisper of silence breathes
from the enclosure.

Walking On Ahead Alone

On an October afternoon,
hiking to the idyllic hill where cattle are grazing,
I take a fork in the river valley
and climb next to a pasture and stone wall.

Higher and higher I climb to the summit
that speaks with the voices of Neolithics
around the fire.
The landscape seems so old, unoccupied.
The road turns around the brow of the hill.
My heart keeps throbbing. Stones settle
over the path.
A rusted iron-hinge gate creaks open.

Not much daylight left.
Bejeweled dragonflies skim the river.
A heavy wind bends the trees,
Where does the path turn?
I plod on, climb higher on flat slabs
of rock next to large upright boulders.
Early settlers must have laced the rocks
for a group burial ground.

A splendid viewing place to await the next life.
He was here, she was here, I'm still here.
Twilight mirages rise above the waterline.
The trek becomes daunting with twists and turns.
I fear not finding my way home.

Jake's Journey

My ski cap and wool jacket
are my concessions to cold weather.
I'm unmoored from what could have been.
If I could tell you-
well, you would want to come with me.

The misty net of terrestrial white light
blankets the sky from horizon to horizon.
I'm a refugee at heart since the loss of my mother.
When she died, my travels began.

Now, I leave the campsite,
follow the sun's movement
through the day with the rhythm
of water tumbling and spraying.

Stillness follows.
The day soaks into my skin
like a memory tattoo as I climb
to crest the ridge's sky decks.

I hike the winding path
up Acadia Mountain at dusk,
dream of saving
the threatened ruffed grouse
in its woodland home.

Wispy shapes under canopies
weave through the forest.
Deer move through trees
like ghostly images.

A Frog? Where?

Morning begins as Arethusa, goddess of spring
arrives. Water lilies clear as ruby red, rose pink
and blossom yellow mingle with pond reeds.

Hiding under the hummock of spartina,
the little gleaming green frog sings
vesper songs. Above, two Golden-crowned kinglets
flash crowns, pursue bejeweled dragon flies in a wildlife
banquet alive with calls revered by Monet.
The sun plays over the pond like sounds of a Mozart harp.

Pristine evolution embodied in water lilies
growing in a murky pond.
I gently pick up the green frog's fragile body
pulsing his breath across my clipped hand,
as he squirms away and gyrates down
to his kingdom, trilling to seduce a female
among the pickerel weeds.

Where the Skunk Goes at Night

Toward darkness, I roll my wheelchair
down the rehab corridor surrendering
to my disability while gazing out the glass door.
A breeze lifts the crisp, green rhododendrons.
From inside, I watch a striped skunk with two babies
saunter out from her domain.

She knows her way, as I do not.
Snowy white fur stripes on her black back
and head, like color of swans' feathers.
I do not want a closer encounter
and she does not want to waste her musk.
She does not know
that the great horned owl over in the trees
does not have a sense of smell.

She raises her black and white tail to the chipmunk
who is squirreling away some of her ants.
I love seeing her bustle
around the little hollow of azalea shrubs.
Her babies curl up holding the breath of summer.
She hollows a puddle hiddey...

Unaware of my watching, she shimmies around
in the little bathtub, rubbing her body and snout clean,
then scrubs her babies. Time breaks away,
the sunset stands still under the bulbous moon
and the great horned owl floats overhead.

Oak Tree Monarch

Across the road from the red barn, the oak tree reigns
on the granite uplands of our East Andover farm.
In spring, the canopy unfolds with Baltimore Orioles
and warblers that skip and flit from branch to twigs.

In summer, near lichen soft nest,
humming birds with rapidly thrumming hearts
glow like flying jewels.
From its branches, I smell the scent of grass at dawn
and hay at dusk.

Eating another apple from the orchard
I love to ride the tire swing as high as it will go.
In the fall, I climb to a crook in the oak and build
a secret clubhouse.
At night, I look into its branches through my window
hoping it protects me from witches and evil spirits.

Growing older, another season, I leave my mark
on the tree
and trek away to find a new age
of kaleidoscopic possibilities.

Cedars of Lebanon

Here where mountaintops snare clouds floating
in from the Mediterranean, we saunter
through the cathedral arched forests
of cedars. Once vast, used for temples and palaces
across Assyria, Persia, Babylon, Egypt and Lebanon.
They enhanced the territory of the Bible
where Jesus revealed himself to his followers.

Enormous trees seem as high as the Cliffs of Babylon
spill light through tracery of limbs.
Some stand alone with distinctive shapes,
others insinuate themselves into relations
with neighbors offering their majesty.
Lines of solid branches crosshatch trunks
seeding roots into craggy limestone.

Branches in tiers sway in the wind like May Pole dancers.
Oval blue-green cones break open to scatter seeds.
Fragrant with balsam perfumed resin,
the cedar trees intertwined with history of 10,000 years.
Now they must migrate up the mountains
to higher altitudes chasing the cold winters they need
to escape warming, the conflicts of war lords
and colonizers of history.

Emissaries of the parade of civilizations
and what we owe them, Cedars of Lebanon
tremble. They have seen the past, will
they see the future?

Pilgrimage to Beatrix Potter's Farm

So take the time and follow me
in April, May or June.
Lift the style and cross over the wall
to the wide Lake District landscape.
Windermere streams dip with morning mist
turning pale rose under the sun.
Snowdrops run wild, elbow their way
into the clot-of-gold crocuses.
Return to your childhood of fairy caravans,
Floppy, Mopsy, Jemina Puddle-duck,

Tommy Tiptoes and Peter Rabbit raiding carrots.
There's a scene in the wildflower meadow
that we could paint of grand open woodlands
full of noble trees. Upon the fells, the wild daffodils
grace the torrent of azaleas down into the valley
and up to the farms. Beatrix Potter plants
for each season: pansies, peas, foxgloves, columbine,
black currants and strawberries.
Here the seasons ferment like a crock of cider.
Pluck some apples from her trees in the orchard.
Then come with me to watch the herds
of Herdwick sheep and hear cuckoos
call from the woods. The sun warms the witch hazel
with its astringent, spicy scent.
Let us watch as Potter pours her heart
into every animal, fruit and flower.

Ever Living Trees, Coast Redwoods

See them looming from far away!

I walk along the worn path answering

the lure for a closer view

of the grove of gigantic trees,

glimpse the sky between

the high branches.

Needles pulse.

Clouds above billow below heaven.

Cinnamon colored

giant redwoods

stand straight and taller

than anything else in the world,

each year adding a layer of sapwood

as the Dawn Redwoods their kin, I plant.

Fog rolls in as I look up.

A hairy woodpecker rat-a-tat-tat-ing

rocks holes for insects.

A chestnut warbler sings silvery songs.

Chihuly Speaks

When a kid, I picked up bits of glass and shells
along the beach.
The translucency shows glass' real character
as frozen liquid. The molecules held in suspension
stimulate the rhythms and forces of life.

Hooked on glass blowing, I'm using the same tools
that are about 2,000 years old. Fusing bits of glass,
I weave the pieces into tapestries.

I love the sensation of vivid colors,
such as cobalt and ruby mixed together,
delicate and thin- walled blues, pinks and grays.

I melt some stain glass in a *glory hole* kiln
twisting and rotating the steel pipe into it. Shapes
of delicate glass glow from above and below.

With a team of artists, the glass magicians,
you can create more original designs.
My *gaffers* are the keys to my creations.
They come from all over the world
traveling from holy lands of glass blowing.

I blow into the pipe, make a collection of bubbles
and bang them with a paddle to beat them up.
Creating chandeliers,

*Chihuly is an American glass sculptor and
entrepreneur. His works are considered
unique to the field of blown glass moving it
into the realm of large-scale sculpture.*

we blow the glass shapes, put them all together;
take apart and reassemble.
The Ruby Red Icicle Chandelier
dangles like a deep-red sea octopus.
The colorful strands of *Mille Fiore* billow
and shine with exotic colors.

In a glass workshop in Seattle, we blow together
bubbles of glass and sail them in a pond;
blow a glass forest with stripes of water flowing
and wind blowing, with swaying creatures of the sea.
My best pieces compare to what Tiffany did.

II
I add separate parts to pieces, the *Ikebana* series
like Venetian forms. Working with blown glass
in sculptured way, we cut, grind, sandblast, acid wash,
stretch glass into dimpled and wavy seashell forms.
I like to have my pieces with splotches of color seem
as if the waves from the ocean moved them around.
My blown baskets change into undulating forms
invoking underwater sea life.
The Niijima floats, large glass spheres, were inspired
by small Japanese fishing boats.

I tell my crew, *"You don't know how far you can go until
you go too far. Push it further and make it bigger!"*
The material and the blowing of glass draws us in.
Hallowed sand and molten glass just keep flowing
as I travel all over the globe.

Woodland Ephemerals

"And for all this, nature is never spent; /there lives the dearest
freshness deep down things..." — *Gerard Manly Hopkins*

In copses of oak, beech and pine,
sown with stars, delicate bluets mark the ground,
host to butterflies and fritillaries.
They skip and glide, slip and dine.

Marsh marigolds, harbingers
inscribe in golden threads in wet meadows
where red-winged blackbirds stoop to drink
luminescence from sepals.

Rusty leaves trail along the ground, hug clusters of tube faces.
Chalices of pink trailing arbutus,
where *Aphrodite* changed *Myrrha* to a myrrh tree,
resin for incense.

Rose azaleas, Emerson's *Rhodora* sweep
across the hill and celebrate
with crimson sap,
beacons for bumble bees.

Faithful to location, bloodroot
of icy-white flowers and golden stamens
seep blood-red sap. *Persephone*
hovers over fragile blossoms.

Hiding from view, green and purple
Jack-in-the-pulpit lifts its sheath,
and serenely preaches. The spadix changes sex
and blooms, whispers intertwined possibilities.

Hiking the Rugged Shore

Hike the land to fulfill a lasting bond
with the peninsula's finger tips
where fresh water of the Sheepscot River
shimmies its tentacles to Muscongus Bay.
My father's Yankee fishing village slides out below.
Islands link out, one ahead of the other,
trailing berries of red and sea-foam bayberry.

Walk terraced steps, taste wild blueberries.
After the coniferous forest, duck under a swing bridge
and leave your pain-riven world behind.
Close to Thunder Hole, ocean booms
against a boulder-piled, jagged shoreline.
Barnacles feather out on intertidal rocks
and fiddler crabs scuttle to shelter in seaweed.

When sunset comes, gaze at the deep blue bay.
Listen to the water thrush's harmony
and I'll try not to leave this place of beauty
where sister and daughter, lost family I love
will be waiting.

Woodland Salamanders in the Microcosmos

In early spring the landscape is awash
with the smell of water, earth and misty air
when a primordial life force burrows out
of the dank earth to the nearby pond.
You will find northern, spotted
and red-backed salamanders — quiet,
nimble, delicate as snow drops —
hiding beneath mossy stones,
rare, hidden and unadorned.

Turn over the stone and pick one up,
a glistening black creature with bright
yellow spots, sand-colored grains,
long tailed, with ridge on top.
A miracle of eternity revealed
as you gently hold its fragile body,
trying to sense the breath of its skin
flowing across your cupped palm.

She swivels and shimmies,
rhythmic like an eel, swerving tiny fingers
and hind limbs to free itself
and squirm away.
She knows how to slip below
the surface of an egg-laying adventure
and live an orderly, purposeful life.
She does not need to conjure up a spell
or send out a sound,
as she gyrates down
in her honorary kingdom.

A Light Shines Here

1985 photo of Wonalancet Union Chapel, New Hampshire
with White Mountain National Forest in the background.

A burst of white as the church stands
surrounded by laurel on the wood's edge.
A wood thrush above in a sheltering tree
sings out its rich vesper song:
Come to me, come to me, I am here, I am here
I step into a soft and silvery retreat
from a great spoil of the sun's natural light.

In this tiny world of a larger universe,
organ music echoes like the call of the brook that runs
down the mountain's range. Immortal lichen and moss
spread on the rocks so the darkness won't fall too heavily.
Western sunlight extends overhead
circling inside my being.

The iridescence of the church reflects the ivory
of time-tested faith strengthened
over hundreds of years.

Inside there is a kind of seamstress of souls,
senders and receivers of earth and star energies,
the intermediaries between our worlds
and the invisible one of another.

Rhythms are geared to the alignment
of earth, moon, and the Northern Crown,
Corona Borealis. I hear the angels sing
as they collect the life force
and spread it panoramically into the kingdom.

American Lotus in the Estuary

Where water and land meet the sky
along the Carolina delta fed by many rivers,
cattails blow in the wind through marsh grass.
A swamp settles among hardwood forest
home to rare species and a station
for migrating birds.

Here, I find the swaying creamy yellow flowers
of American Lotus
rising above floating pads of saucer-like foliage.
Water pearls across high-stock petals of each bloom
reaching for the sun.
I call to mind the lotus eaters
who shared their flower food with Odysseus' sailors
those who tasted it lost their longing for home.
Within the deep golden centers of white-tipped stamens,
lotus bees buzz above the lapping water.

Far from my home today,
I linger here in timeless moments
and lose my longing to return home.

Finding the Gingko Tree

Because it holds the generative core of life, we learn from it.
Nourished by spring rains and sun baths
It radiates a redolence of rays.

Male sperm cells wiggle and swim from catkins,
make their way to the female tree
and join ovaries.

Green-gray lichen and reindeer moss home in on the bark.
Silver-apricot colors the lobed shaped leaves.

Saved by Buddhist monks on Deshima Island.
Some lived on after the atomic blast of Hiroshima.
Near the epicenter of the explosion
"No more Hiroshimas" carved on one's temple.

Golden leaves nourish the inner tree, keep it alive through stormy
    seasons
and hide the tiny nest of the ruby-throated hummingbird,
interwoven with thistledown.

Maidenhair flows in the dark when the sun is gone.

Hiking and Humming in Acadia

The sky implausibly blue over rose-beige granite
laced with black dolerite
over carriage roads and stone bridges,
crossing birch, spruce, beech forests
and expansive meadows on the shore path.

Walking the ocean park loop,
we traverse the bluffs rising above
the purple-blue sea,
dropping down from cobble cliffs,
over boulders carved and chiseled.
Stepping over mossy hummocks,
we skirt Jordan Pond and Eagle Lake
around Thunder Hole where foaming waves
rush and ricochet into the fissure.
Once a rogue wave crashed
over many visitors
knocking them down.

My friend wants to linger to collect sea shells.

Jewel-toned wood nymphs hide in pitch pine
and red spruce forests among layers
of sweet cinnamon fern.

Peregrine falcons' wings shadow skyward,
nest on the 1000 ft. high cliff
and harass red-tailed hawks.

A bell buoy clangs, rolls in the swells.
The ocean serenades as we continue,
reaching the tree-less summit,
grand finale of Cadillac Mountain
where we hope to meet the Wabanakiis.

Marginal Way, Ogunquit

Mid-morning fog lifts. My daughter and I
bound together from different spheres,
feel pull of the moon on ocean's tide.
on rocky outcrops heaving out of coast
on cliffs where glaciers gouged retreat.
We pause on pathway, sit on the bench
as my sister and I once did
sharing Coleridge's
The Rime of the Ancient Mariner.
Today dwellings slope to hidden beaches,
and children explore tidal pools of slate-blue
mussels and rosy crabs in flotillas
of seaweed. Wary of slick-covered
downward slanting boulders,
a giant snail's trail, we view
the ocean's glow of cobalt blue
writhing away to the horizon. My daughter's hair
glistens with sunlight as my sister Beverly's.
I breathe the essence of wild roses
and beach plums covering rocks.
Crashing surf in high swells
sounds against domes of granite and schist.
Hymns emerge from shrubbery
as swallow-tailed piping plovers wearing
black stripes on shoulders
come soaring in on ocean tides
whistling their lonely notes.
Plovers flutter in circles and cuddle on rocky cliffs,
feathered wings clutching mates and chicks;
seeking green urchins that puff up spines
like porcupines. They anchor themselves to rocks
in ocean water, clear as quartz crystal
flowing in tidal pools, most potent amber.

The Spirit Bear of Canada

They are Kermodes belonging to the territory
of the Klemoth people.
In the great Bear Rainforest, a crow sounds
clarion caws and alerts the animals to our arrival.
A glowing female bear, sacred to local tribes,
shifts her weight of 300 pounds
and waddles into the Salmon River.

Numinous with full honey-hued hair,
she snatches and bats a rose-pink salmon.

Her first year-of-life cub
sports a fur collar and white-brown coat.
There is no male to take the cub down,
so mother and cub slip into the pool.

The cub studies us curiously, sniffs us out
and devours the wrapped in seaweed
flesh of the batted salmon.
Mother eats the brains and eggs.

Snapping our cameras as for celebrities,
we wait frozen with rapture,
flooded with reverence
for the legacy of mother and her cub.

Flowing Southward

For three months, from woodlands
of the Northeast
sunrise to sundown, hawk watchers
at Lighthouse Point Park
record the southward autumn spectacle
from tributaries
that join to form a river.
Between us and the clouds
they sweep onward in the vanguard
of migration!

Tens of thousands, stars of the show,
friendly broad-winged hawks,
maneuver through clouds and
chase fleeing prey.
The sharp-shinned hawks with rounded wings
and long tails, blue-gray above, rusty stripes below
boil up in huge kettles on the way to Latin America.
Unmatched kestrels fly with power
slip speedily through thermals
and soar on currents of air
harassed by swallows.
Merlins from boreal forests
blast low across dunes, pursuing songbirds.
Peregrine falcons fastest on earth,
masters of deep dives speed at 175 mph
to brackish marshes.
Winter's breath moves them along!
A smorgasbord of red-tailed hawks and eagles
swoop in on an updraft.

St. Francis of Assisi

On a brisk night in late September
someone didn't flick off the artificial lights
when the veil of darkness scattered
over earth. Birds soaring on currents of air
pulled down by a great whirlwind
that caught them in a vortex.

A migration spectacle of flowing birds
fluttered down from northern woods:
warblers, thrushes, tanagers, buntings
orioles, kingbirds, meadowlarks.
A galaxy of dazzling shades splashed
with ultramarine, indigo, golden,
iridescent blues and greens
with shining golden eyes.
St Francis knew them all.

Companions full of agility and stamina
carried messages of grace from rivers,
mountains and woods.
All once skimmed the limitless skies
sending out warbling voices and wailing cries.
Under urban lights, thousands of exhausted
migrants struck glass, collided
falling like leaves in a jeweled rain forest
splattering below high-risers and skyscrapers.

Once, they shared a universal language
so much to say, so much music,
so many choruses left unsung.

Landbirds' Migration

When the moon is full,
wind whistles over the restless sea
carrying songbirds
in dramas of life and death.

The flocks, bolstered by breeding,
fly by night.
Waves of warblers, vireos, thrushes,
and sparrows on epic journeys,
some non-stop
along the Atlantic coast line
from New England
to South America
over landscape shaped
by bodies of water,
winds, lands and time.

I hear the songbirds drop call their notes
before they reveal themselves.
In hues of carmine, gold, sapphire,
emerald, brown, ebony, orange and white,
and less colorful hues of fall leaves.
Sojourners in marvelous array
illuminating the season
inscribing their poetry.

By the light of a dying fire,
I wish them Godspeed along their way.

Nature's Widescreen Light Show

Whispered about in darkness,
a mystery ancients recorded in sacred books,
aurora borealis written in logs of forgotten ships
sunk to the bottom.
Early settlers saw the lights
as gay polka dancers
and Alaskan Athabaskan perceived
sky dwellers, spirits of the dead
sending messages.

Shared with visitors across midnight,
many travelers come
to watch aurora borealis in the deepest,
coldest regions of the planet's reach of space.
In wonder, their eyes open to the night sky
as gossamer rays unfold.
Multi colors and bright-magenta flash and flicker,
erratic as the wind, incandescent meteors of lights
blaze and sway.
They follow some unseen authority,
a power humans will never command.

Faster than eyes can follow, behind shadows
of mountains, colors drape, dash and sweep.
The hunters then felt communion across the ages
with travelers and mystics who were awestruck
by ghostly lights in the sky.
Auroras illuminate the moon
hanging over the mountains.
Bright waves of light shimmer around the sky,
fade into the heavens through the shroud of mist.

Old-Growth Giant Sequoias of the Forest

Sequoia named after son
of a Cherokee chief's daughter,
older than the English language
delirious of size, elephantine,
more than 8000 in the giant forest.
I cannot comprehend their height.
They inspire reverence and recalibrate
my sense of time and space.

Feel the trunk, a reddish-orange glow
grayish-brown branches
crooked and gnarled.
A road passes through.
Tourists who travel from afar
pose for photos.

Pacific tree frogs live in caverns of the trunk
like grottos of a sea cliff.
A bubbling ball of brown feathers
launches from a treetop nest
onto a tiny purple cone.
The voice of the sequoia forest sings with:
a varied thrush's flutelike whistles
the rustle of wind passing
through branches and
the sway of tree trunks.
It buzzes with crickets sounding
and Clark's nut catchers breaking cones.

All reflect the power of wind, ice, snow, rock and sun.
I want to ask their blessings
remember how the Dawn Redwood, a cousin
towers over my backyard.
Who would have believed sequoias could live
for thousands of years?

Millennium Grove, R.I.P

Giant sequoias, Temples of Time,
I offer you fragrant frankincense,
for thousands of years of growth
in your forests
of cedar, Douglas fir, Sitka spruce,
and ponderosa pine.

Ferns genuflect under forest columns
in under canopy like priests swinging
braziers of burning myrrh.
You were seedlings, saplings and shoots
when Neolithics lugged giant
stones for Stonehenge.

Groves of ancestors sheltered
nomadic wanderers;
now a crown of branches cradle
a pair of rare murrelets
sending out whistling
cadences to the heavens.
You hold spotted owls,
offer shelter to salamanders
and save spawning salmon.
Then your limbs are lopped off
and song sparrows are bloodied
silenced in their nest.
A revving of chainsaws storms
your temples as trees plunge
and smash forest-loving creatures.

Earthmovers come, chain the stripped
arms, pull trunks up by roots,
strip from the site. You're scavenged
to a chip mill that grinds your temples
up for pulp.

Germany's Black Forest Reverie

*"If we surrendered to earth's intelligence we could rise
up rooted, like trees." — Rainer Maria Rilke*

I love hiking through Germany's Black Forest,
a haven where memories of holidays and childhood
emerge from a repository of traditions and time.

Drunk with legends, I know this forest
is sacred as if a god descended
on the highest of mountains.

A series of groves envelop me in silver-sheen foliage.
Fairies, gnomes, trolls and witches conjure
where the Grimm brothers found their inspiration
for fairy tales, *Hansel and Gretel,*
and *Little Red Riding Hood.*

When I gaze up in the canopy of dense fir trees,
the sky appears like a stream of tributaries
winding through the forest.
A spicy, resinous fragrance fills the air.

The forest birds, woodpeckers, owls, warblers
love this place with centuries'- old fir trees
for building nests. I hear their quirky calls
as they perch overhead,
eyes pinned to the nests they build.

The forest hums with life
as cuckoo clocks hand carved in the village
rhythmically sing.
I feel these surroundings with all my senses.

Love, I'll Try Again

Years, escaping from my wounding path of pain
I revisit blessed ones I have lost and think of them
with Sunday-sermon reverence
that lengthens spring days with Easter lilies
unfailing visits to grave sites.
I did not think I'd have enough love to give again.

The daffodils and crocuses are unfurling.
He picks some purple hyacinths,
places them in a wooden wheelbarrow
on the patio near the glass door
fills it with soil and waters them
putting out water for the tree swallows
and robins that flit down
from the birdhouses he made.

In the woods, painted turtles slip and slide in rush
to vernal pools.
The red- winged blackbirds call in the rise
above the snow that sinks further into the roots
of scarlet maples.
Wild blood root emerges from dead leaves
along the stone walls like candles sheltered
from a soughing wind.
A great blue heron hitches a ride
on a suite of thermals.

My body resonates in the hollows of my hips.
Dawn begins and we go outside to see
the canopy of stars
and touch the galaxy in many directions.

I Did Not Think

*"So constant is the changing tide
Where sea and shore and time collide." — Jane Yolen*

I would find love again in my town
by the Sound along the Hammonasset River
where the rare oystercatchers visit
below the rocks. Driftwood trees
and glacial boulders inscribe
with a druid's labyrinth.

A fire touches him as it does me.
Flames of incandescence
fluttering like a migrating monarch.
The sky shines in argentine gloss.

My mind, an hourglass watching
as we navigate our 70s,
play carefully around the edges.
The new moon extends waxing
in the evening sky.

We meet on separate spheres
like a sliding timeline.

Gossamer parachutes rouse our spirits.
A changing juncture
transforming neglected fields
into green refuges.

The Parts of You That Only I Know
Bow to e.e. cummings, (1923-1997)

Black-grey hair curls, green-gray eyes,
slender, no tattoos. You rock me
and gather my energy.
Your voice clear, laconic, and strong leaves
messages every day.

You fend for yourself in 1733 rental house
16 years, some dates with a few women,
never wanting to avenge the slight of divorce
or visit a therapist for that sadness.

Under the same moon, we love the beauty of beaches
combing the seashore for shells to take home.
I see dead robin fish from red tide.
We both view purple, pink sunsets taking a long walk.

You look at clouds like a meteorologist
predicting "warm days, strong winds, brilliant sunsets"
and cherish the love of the men's club,
for men only, that holds you.

Your luscious kiss that never holds back,
libido less body sleeps next to mine
I need a key to unlock what you're thinking
The shaft of light in a dark room
the celestial glow from the open window
on the roof.

Driving to Florida Through All Seasons

Starting out, fragile and uncertain.
North winds blowing to scurry the leaves
and stars spreading, leave behind the daylight.
Fortressed in a blue Ford truck
as hurricane rains pummel.
My friend and I each foresee a different journey.
Two minds, for me an adventure, for him a destination.
I caught my breath as rain and fog spread invisibility.
In the passenger seat I engage in following maps.
The traffic dissects conflicted sentences.
Kenn Morr Band plays *Higher Ground*.

Rain in slabs of high tide flow over the truck
and four lanes of traffic interweave.

In some southern states landscapes lie barren
with slivers of tall cypresses and hardwoods
slashed to sparseness.
Hanging moss covers the *hammock* pines
in the Carolinas.
Logged forests turn to fields of fog.
I wonder what he is reflecting on.

Closer to destination, mirrors of intercoastal
waterways ripple million dollar yachts.
With the driver's strong hands on the wheel,
we arc across
the Caloosahatchee River.
And still I see thin, translucent branches
against hazy sky
held fast by twisted trees fading
into taller ones.

PART II

Cruising on Old Father Rhine

I walk on deck to the full moon
    feeling Emerson's
haunting power of water and shadows.
        I am missing loved ones and feel strange, alone.
All around me is the closeness of couples.

Dawn begins as the sun spills
    over the Rhine.
In the Swiss Alps brooks flow
    braiding glacial streams.
The river filters across rugged terrain over boulders
    from basements of time.
I know how infinitesimal I am now.
Storm petrels shuffle in the air
    and become wind borne.
Castles peer down on half-timbered houses.
    Passing the river maiden's Lorelei Rock that lures
sailors, I absorb my aloneness.

We cruise through the Wachau Valley,
    past monastery ruins, wine-growing villages
from Celtic and Roman times. I learn the language of loss.
    The river flows through meadows and forests
by mountain chains with snow on summits.

Gracing the villages, terraced vineyards
    of Rhine and Riesling climb cliffs. Mown grass
lies out to dry in the sun. My wandering heart
    visits flower-strewn pastures.

Sweet-lilting melodies enfold from abbeys.
    I steel myself, as my past and present coexist
in foreign landscape peopled with strangers.

Great Bear Lake

straddles the Arctic Circle
stretches endlessly to the horizon,
     essentially primeval.
     You once could drink its pure water. Now it flows in our veins.
Slate-blue curtains of mist rise above white snow crystals.

     Saved as the Last Supper by Leonardo Da Vinci
Hearing the keepers, the lake calls us to prayer
     Sitting, we listen to aboriginal elders
     lead the Gospel and Rosary.
When did the lake welcome such possibilities
     and accommodate so many.

II
Silence pervades northern lights glisten.
     A lake trout leaps out of the water by an abandoned
     beaver lodge. Ptarmigan and pine marten, musk ox,
caribou, moose and bear animate its infinity.
     Beyond,
thickets of untouched boreal forest sanctify.
     Hoarfrost sparkles on undersides of needles.
The elders say, *people from the South will come to the last refuge*
     that gives life
          to all lakes and oceans.
When there is no food or water
     around the world,
          all of humanity will come here

At sunset the moon appears in blue-black sky.

*One of the ten largest lakes in the world; the world's first UNESCO
Biosphere Reserve to be led by an indigenous community. Bear lake
people (Sahtuto'ine) are the keepers.*

Hiking in Provence

Uphill and downhill we trek
all morning as the sun
shines in persimmon color from the West
to medieval fortress town, La Palud
surrounded by copses of olive trees.

Resting on our blanket,
we spread our cornucopia:
a wheel of goat cheese,
sauces of goose paté,
garden-ripe tomatoes,
snipped basil,
and loaves of crusty bread
sipping Provençal Vin Rouge
like *Picnic in the Grass.*

Gardens below the tree line
show their spicy herbs
of rosemary, thyme and tarragon.
I sample and pass around the green
Benedictine Liquor of the Monks.
Everywhere apple-red poppies,
gold broom and amethyst lavender.
Below limestone peaks
in the pasture some cows
with up-rolled eyes
are eating the wild flowers.

I gaze down knowing why Manet,
Van Gogh and Cezanne painted here.

"Life itself began in the sea, so each of us begins
his individual life in a miniature ocean..." — Rachel Carson

On The Atlantic Island Queen

off the Maine coast watching
for humpback whales
beneath an eye-bright sky
hoping to chance upon the mysterious
astonishing giants of the world
and the best long-distance swimmers.

They seem noble as they travel in pods,
jets spouting
coasting around us on the ship,
body surfing with graceful flippers.
I see their translucent, silver-bright bodies
and hear the rushing sounds of breathing
as they race and hide in the bow waves
inscribing their sleek bodies on the surfaces.

Masters of the commute embark on the longest
migration in the world.
Miraculously, nursing whales
follow their mothers' medley of groans,
moans, roses and snores,
through the crackling of coral and currents.
Humpbacks sing and whistle as their hearts
beat and pulse with the rhythms of countless
sea creatures.

Eelgrass Forest in Long Island Sound

As the golden orb draws back seawater,
I snorkel in slinky motion
around branches

looking at undersea meadows like hay fields.
Stroked gently by breezes the Prius of gardens
emerald, golden and brown.

A sanctuary for drifting motes
of copepods ricocheting, unfolding arms
draped in sarong seaweeds.

In this home, rock crabs hunker down.
Clams spout fountains; rose-colored starfish
bloom. Seahorse families

curl and retreat into depths. Eelgrass extends
its influence; another nursery for scarce
species of larvae and fish, cafeteria

for diatoms, algae, and flagellates entwining.
Making leaps of faith, mummichogs and pipefish
suck up dinners from ribbon-like blades

of flower spikes; pass on to the next customer
along the food links. Arctic brant devour dinner
to fortify 3000 mile trek to Mexico.

So come with me, take in the sights before
they vanish. One gigantic leap of evolution,
the journey that has brought me here.

Atlantic Salmon of the Penobscot

Silver birches grace the meadows.
Below tundra of stunted willows and beech
hilltops, above the *Rhine Of Maine,*
the river sparkles silver with the king of fish,
Atlantic salmon.
Hundreds of thousands ride the ocean currents
migrating among boulders and ledges,
to anchor their flesh in stony gravel.

Golden-orange salmon eggs slumber in gravel beds.

Here from distant feeding grounds,
smolts trek downstream with siblings,
swim the Penobscot, move at night
and bunker down during the day,
defying damns, currents, tide and gravity;
many are snatched by bears, bald eagles
and cormorants.
For many centuries, they fed
Passamaquoddy, Micmacs,
and Wabanaki tribes.

Later, for a hundred years, our salmon
disappeared into obsidian pollution while anglers
and natives testified, protested and grieved.

Then in the 70s fealty brought some salmon back.
Tails crossing the surface, they twisted, jumped,
tossed, and swirled all the way from Greenland
bookmarking bone-deep scents along the way.
People came to watch in awe and Ted Williams
returned to fish.
The pull is so strong, salmon must not stray
far from their home stream.
Family lineage returns and sounds of water
rush over stone beds.

Sea Shepherds
"It's a credit to the species to be here at all." — *Todd McLeish*

In northern region of Koluctoo Island,
far above the Arctic Circle, I took a journey
to see strange sea creatures of a long spiral tusk
and ice and whale, cherished as unicorns.

Couples click and squeak in dolphinese—a serenade
of gurgles, mood, grunts, and creaky barks,
then flip with reverberations squirting me.

Each, five hundred pounds, backs like steel cables,
traveling in pods and nerds near the Godzilla Iceberg.
Most revered, horned serpents gamboling,
crossing spiral horns above glossy bodies.

Some Narwhals lift flukes, rumps and heart-shaped tails
and gracefully swim and dive in unison
in crests of waves under the orange-glow sun.
They rear their spiral horns as in fencing.

Quickly they dive fifteen hundred meters deep,
more than twenty times a day, a round trip
to dine on jellyfish, flat fish and krill.
A pair of body surfs the breakers
with tusks reaching toward the sky.

For dinner, I declined the narwhal steak, a delicacy.
When asked to dine with the Inuits, I ordered the muktuk.

Japanese Honeysuckle

From Japan and Korea,
in America it began by the Potomac River.
Now ubiquitous
vast lands and every continent.

Intoxicating fragrance of cream-colored
blossoms announced from miles away.
Night flying hawk moths and hummingbirds
from hundreds of yards come to distill nectar.
Shafts of sunlight filter through its dense leaves.
Bee groups forsake other plants
and come humming in its foliage.
Thrushes sing a chorus of possibilities in leaves.

Naturalists consider it a menace, troublesome
and do not welcome the sweet-smelling outsider.
Many labor to eradicate it.
I am bewildered by its heady aroma.

Meddling with plants, we rejoice over them,
smell their fragrance and call them invasive.
Ambiguity embodied in a flowering shrub.

Green Frogs Appear in Backyard Pond

I remember, when I was young, I scooped a bucketful
of pollywogs and brought them home
watching over time their metamorphosis
as they grew legs.

Now older and retired I build a
granite-rimmed circulating pond
and a waterfall
filled with water lilies inside and red primroses
around rocks.

Six large spotted frogs stare in peaceful repose,
through rich green algae, bubbles,
and lily pads.

Two swim in elegant strokes, legs outstretched
sleekly as an arrow. They create subtle ripples
like movement of water striders
on the surface.

One hops among the lily pads
in classic compact leaps. Other peers
from a bed of lacy algae
flashing its gold-rimmed bronze eyes.

I visit this enchantment another day.
The gregarious creatures peer with protruding eyes.
from the rim of the pool.
I'm glad all the frogs haven't lost their legs
and have the proper number of limbs.

Leap From Grace

Frank dug out my backyard pond
and encircled with field rocks,
planted yellow day lilies and blue irises.

I'm delighted when green frogs arrive twanging
their voices.
Later, a new olive-green bullfrog with bubbly skin
flashes golden eyes and pulses his tympanic membrane.

Calling nonstop *jug-o-rum, jug-o-rum* all day and night,
the huge bullfrog sporting long hind legs lords over all.
Koi and froglets snuffle in the depths.
He jumps on a green lily pad, quickly bolts
like a coiled snake and stretches out
his arms with three fingers.
When colorful butterflies visit pond side flowers,
he traps them into his voracious mouth.

A hummingbird comes in close to gather nectar
and he snags it too.
He takes pleasure surfing and patrolling
for butterflies and other small birds.
Often, he rides green females until they drown.

I am horrified to have the bullfrog
destroy my pond biosphere.
Blood-chilled, I want to change the bullfrogs' evolution.

Frogs Key to Life

We can learn from frogs in their vast array
of size and color proliferating.
As large as a Galapagos turtle,
as small as a grain of rice.
First inhabitants of the Earth to have a voice,
make themselves known, to leave
a water lifestyle and colonize Devonian land.

All have niches in different homesteads:
Asian horned frogs are camouflaged like dead leaves
on forest floors.
Golden-poison darts and orange ones are festooned
with brown blotches.
A blue-jean frog decorated with painted dots carries
tiny tadpoles on her back up a tree to bromeliad plants.
A canary yellow frog with bulbous shining eyes
submerges her tadpoles.
A burgundy-colored frog pulsates with pink veins on its belly.
Hour glass frogs splattered with irregular white circles
gather poison from beetles they eat.
All look painted by numbers and Jackson Pollock.

Icons of primeval forests, they practice arias in the trees.
Some frogs' choruses bubble like rivers of sound.
Others croak plaintively and leap out of view.
In our time, pools of frogs belly-up,
speak for the quiet majority.
When frogs are fruitful and multiply,
the more heavenly our lives.

Guillermo del Toro's Film, The Shape of Water
A horror-monster, musical- jailbreak-period-spy romance

The Actuality of Loneliness

Eliza, my friend lives alone next
to her failed artist neighbor
who feeds her Key-lime pie, my favorite.
We have lizard-green tongues

She speaks with sign language
and cleans house in a science lab.
I work with her.
At work, we meet a creature with toad-like skin
who breathes underwater and in air.
He has arms and legs and no tail,
like an Amazonian beast.
Gills palpitate around his neck.
Kept in a tank, the god swims even though scientists
tether him with an iron collar and chains.
The creature is tortured persistently
by an electric cattle prod.
A scientist wants to kill him and cut him up.

How heavy my heart is filled with my own losses.
My mind wants to protect and release him.

Eliza wants to organize his escape and live with him.
To her dream man she brings hard-boiled eggs
and bewitches with her dancing.

Fantasy absorbs our waking lives.
In the arms of the god-like creature, Eliza signs,
All that I am, all that I have ever been,
brought me here to you.

Star Viewpoint

After midnight in the fall,
I go out with an astronomer from Audubon
to view the stars vibrating in the sky.
I think of Plato who believed the stars
to be the final destination
of all mortal humans after sojourn on earth.
In the sky I see the Square of Pegasus, with
its four bright stars in the corners.

I imagine the North Pole where the sun
does not rise between September and March
and think of my sister and children who once
lived there.
The first magnitude star Deneb
marks the tail of Cygnus the swan,
who slides down the Milky Way galaxy.
I look to the southern horizon, see the twinkling
red superstar giant Antares, the heart of Scorpios.
Great viewing of Orionid meteor shower on
night time display as Earth passes through a line
of meteoroids left over from Halley's Comet.

Soon the moon will be at perigee,
the closest point to earth with Mars, Mercury, Saturn,
and Venus appearing together.
They guide nonstop
warblers traveling by night
and make me feel connected
to nature and to the cosmos.
All the physical stars seem transcendent
connected to heaven, God, immortality,
and to each other.

Moon Gazing

Tonight, the friendly harvest moon appears
in all its splendor, large, special and brilliant
taking on fiery colors of red and orange
with a human face of eyes, nose, and mouth.

On Flag Hill farm, lightning bugs flicker.

Native Americans thought wolves sang the moon
into existence calling it the wolf moon.
I'm not certain, but I believe some humans transform
into wolves when the moon is full.

I watch it move along parallel with the horizon
seeming bigger than ever as a procession of broad-wing
hawks and peregrine falcons soar over.
Golden eagles join the pass over too in front
of the moon just as the lunar light show
near St Michael's Tower
gives a rare presentation.

Earth and moon align perfectly as the sun
blots out the moon's reflected radiance.

Flowing Reflections, Enders Falls, Granby, CT

Inspiration from Patricia Seacamp's painting
for Madison Art Exhibit, 2018

I do not feel like a silent stone,
I'm nearer to being a river.
A binding thread that transmutes
and reconstitutes
from loving memories of loss,
like water falling over a steep edge
that can't be tamed.

Sometimes I plunge into the rolling crash
of an ocean wave.
Other years, I treasure a piece of driftwood
found in a quiet marsh land.

I have learned to flow
through wilderness.
My waterfalls divide, then merge
separate, vanish, reappear and move
downhill toward the sea.

I am growing and flowing
through woodlands
changing from waterfalls,
rivers, lakes, streams, fog and dew.
The river reflects the splendor
of the woods and its many colors,
kinetic and soothing.
Water always finds its way.

Gifts of the Season

For this sacred time of winter solstice,
snow whispers, drops softly.
Gifts are tucked away underground,
under snow, under stars.

Presents unwrap themselves before
my eyes: morning a sunrise softly silver
with clouds of pearl colors.
Sunsets stretch the day.

Wild birds: scarlet, tawny, rose and olive colored
flash through trees, swooping close.
Signature of mouse prints cross the snow

On the beach waves push up and sweep
push up and sweep against the sand.
Opalescent seashells rise with the tide.

New tides run within me, cycles of sleep
and crystal sharp awareness
keyed to the sun, to the moon, to the universe.

Around lamplights shine halos.
The frost tangles grapevine and bull briar.
Ice crackles, flexes with frozen life
on the pond bottom.

In the woods, under frosted ground,
spore cases reach above velvety-green mosses.
Fiddlehead ferns unchanged
since ancient times prepare for winter.

Endless presents on the ground, in trees
and under stars unwrap themselves.

Wandering in Hammonasset

Above the shore, I watch the great white heron
with gigantic wing span envelop space,
ride the airwaves trailing its slender black legs.
In the moments between sunset and dusk
agile aviators, willets whistle over the sand hills.
A flock of piping plovers cut a dash,
defending their young on the upper shore
running back and forth pretending to be hurt,
trilling high notes.

Alone now, I remember the many times
we explored ocean bays and salt marshes:
collecting sculptures of sea shells,
surveying seals in the river
and once watched a Diamondback Terrapin
cross our path.

At times, I close my eyes to hear the Fiddler Crabs.
Waves of silence between the requiem of the tide
going out, and the time before
the last-light fading.

This is a world that dies, transforms and goes on
under a vast light-streaked sky.
The Hammonasset River twists and curves
seeking its ultimate outlet into the Sound
as air currents going out to sea pass over
Rosa Rugosa.

A Trek in the Winter Woods

"For many years I was the self-appointed inspector of snow storms
and rain storms and did my duty faithfully..." — Henry David Thoreau

The snow has been pouring through the sky,
well below zero, wind chills, forty miles per hour.
Wind blasts at my back and stings my face.

I know this land in all conditions.
My snowshoes sink into fluffy snow.
Snowflakes shake on and powder my clothes.
Gusts drive the snow.
No wood ducks or fish swim in the frozen pond.

Wind roars! Crowns of trees bluster, branches
creek and moan as they bend against each other.
I hear footsteps of animals.
Ruffed grouse is trekking too, using the snow to keep warm,
diving into a snowbank.

I am absorbed by wildness.
The landscape is pure white, shady gray and lustrous black.

A moose spots me. I think we are related.
    Something spiritual happens when our faces meet.
I catch the reflection of its eyes. We recognize
and know each other.

Trees in the Winter Forest

"When I say, 'Trees suckle their children,' everyone knows
immediately what I mean." — Peter Wohlleben Gordon Welters

I
The dynamic winter trees
fan their limbs over all, want to be watched
and listened to. Standing trunk to trunk,
side by side, they protect their neighbors,
with choiring branches that allow the light
to touch all, not blocking other's light.
Admire their crowns against purplish-blue skies.
Inscribing touchstones,
some toss their hair, cut or colored leaves
changing and falling off. They fix wrinkled bark
like humans remaining similar through time.

II
The trees in my forest communicate with neighbors
and discover secrets from their world.
They can count and remember,
nurse neighbors, send electric signals
of danger across fungal networks
and keep other stumps alive.

Deep green moss and lichen grow on their barks,
make flesh, make food, make flowers.
In the winter quietness of the woodlands,
guarded by these stalwart sentinels,
roots intertwine under snow tracks of deer.
And a white-footed mouse loses its life
in the drama of an owl's dinner.
In some level of sun, earth and water, we
are of the same rhythms dropping wealth
as seasons roll by—investing in the long view.

Bigfoot Snowshoeing

I bundle up, buckle my boots, strap on
Algonquin snowshoes,
become as a Willow Ptarmigan.
I set out on snow's ermine mantle,
clamber across the untrammeled icy lake
and over the old abandoned cow roads
into the heart of remote woodlands.
A short-tailed bird pecks its way
down a tree trunk tucking away insects,
then joining the flock of nuthatches.

A ruffed grouse bristles stiff on sides of toes
dives head first into a snow bank.
I drink deeply; feel related to the Pequawkets,
who camped here.

Across the still landscape, I break trail
into the backcountry over wrinkles of snow.
Glide, slide, soar, and whoosh.
In the distance, a panorama
of Arcadian mountains rise.

Iridescent ice crystals rise on the pond.
Snowy Owl visitors come down from the north.
I hush into silence held fast by imagining
the thousands' mile flight of these Arctic creatures.

As I Ebb Toward...

I
On a painted bunting day
as the ferry pulls away from Nantucket,
I spy fish-wielding dolphins,
vaulting out of the sea.
Baby whales follow the songs
of their mothers
seeking milk from their breasts.
And a sperm whale floats in the waves.

II
Gray shingled houses look out
at waves rising and falling.
Around the bay, pink swamp mallows
frame the marsh, use underground
networks to share water
and call to their pollinators.
I stoop to touch mosaic of sea shells
on berm of sand.

I'm swimming in the foam
as waves crest over my head and I float
on to the calmer seashore of Nantucket beach.
Flocks of storm petrels arc up and down and glide
like helicopters over waves.

III
My womb now empty once housed four lives.
Two survived into the baptism of life.
I have lost my place like stones on
the upper beach.

What do I have to latch onto
in the currents and the waves?
Isn't it enough to swim with spiraling surges?
The Great Point light anchors as holdfasts
of giant kelp suspend me.

Hammonasset Reflections

Near Purple Martin Pond, plants thrust, sprout,
along the Moraine Trail among the granite rocks.
Yellow-rump warblers scurry the leaves.
Each season, I birdwatch there, scatter seeds to sustain
nestlings. I am blessed to be close to home
drawing the honey down along the Sound, the place I live.

Friends and visitors shift their worlds to live
here in summer. Naturalists come to see what's sprouting.
Families pitch tents in the campground, make it home
vacation and shoot the breeze among the rocks;
taking children to nature center to help sustain
captive creatures. Sweet smelling roses bloom under leaves.

In spring I look for wildflowers before the tree leaves
appear and watch the killdeer shield nests to keep chicks alive.
Waves of high tide slide over glacier rocks.
From the shore pods of seals splash into the river to sustain
their young to grow like shoots.
Frogs and turtles colonize new habitat close to original homes.

Hammonassets found the river a rich place to call home
I am intimate with each contour and leaf,
diverse creatures living among volcanic rocks
teaching me about every species alive and non-alive.
Tundra of stunted cedar and eucalyptus sprouts
across hilltops into distant feeding grounds sustain

animals. In shallow water during high tide kelp sustains
crabs. Sea anemones add erect arms to move their homes.
They thrust themselves out of the sea like groping sprouts
and change their shapes among glistening leaves
of sea lettuce that chomp chlorophyll to keep alive.
Tannin stalks of ginger sponges attach to rocks.

Large flicks of red knots comb the shores feeding on rocks
whose growth horseshoe crabs' eggs heartily sustain.
Faithfully farmers brought this Edenic garden alive
where foxes, shorebirds and land birds find a home
as other creatures safeguard under layers of leaves.
Some plants lie in wait until spring, mysterious sprouts.

Across tundra of stunted willows and cedar sprout rocks.
Fish, leaves, roots, and plants once sustained Hammonassetts.
Shad, alewives, and bass migrate upstream, longing for home.

The Ultimate Pilgrimage to Hokkaido

Taking the undersea
Seikan Tunnel Railway,
we pass Japanese Archipelago
of Honshu, Shikoku, Kyusho,
and Hokkaido. Mary, my dear friend
was our leader. Fifteen years
younger than I, she died last week.

In nature's ultimate Utopia, Hokkaido,
we stroll seductive paths;
hundreds of tinted species
of flaming hues; reed warblers,
grebes, and honey-colored wagtails
harbor in cryptomeria trees.
Vistas of blooming wildflowers,
orchids, Jacob's ladder,
Japonica trees, camellias, azaleas
cover wide-spreading landscapes.

In Kushiro Shitsugen Park,
meandering rivers,
lakes and wetlands
in twilight gardens
of woodlands, forests and fields.
The bullet train takes us to the avenue
lined with gigantic cypress trees
of Meiji-Jimmy Shinto Shrine.
We enter through Torii Gateway
see the inner gardens with streams of blue,
purple and white iris beds,
royal-blue water lily ponds
and thousands of trees
from all over Japan.

A home for rare species,
the Japanese red-crowned crane,
symbol of fidelity and immortality.

SPECIAL THANKS...

First, my profound thanks to the Guilford Poetry Guild. I am most indebted to the members who have helped me generously when I needed more creative ways of expression who have made this book possible.

I am especially grateful to my supportive fellow poets in the Connecticut Poetry Society: Laura and Victor Altshul and Tony Fusco who have stimulated and critiqued my poems in the last two years.

My deepest thanks, to poet and teacher, Edwina Trentham who has guided me over the last ten years, with good examples, and pushing me harder toward poetic richness and imaginative writing, that helped my book take shape and for her many real sparks of illumination.

I am greatly appreciative of the past editor of *Connecticut Review*, poet and teacher, Vivian Shipley who gave me continual critiques and encouragement in poetry classes over three years that stimulated my poetry to grow with passion, complexity and imaginative leaps.

I thank my publisher Jennifer A. Payne who guided me in printing this book of poems. Receive my gratitude for all the hard work and guidance you have given me. Your attention to every word and detail was most fruitful. Lianna Altieri also helped generously with art, photography, graphics and technology.

Many grateful thanks to my family: Frank Scot, Gail, Alyssa, Lianna, Hannah Altieri and Jessica Hosfeldt, my niece for generous assistance with photography and technology.

Many places I have visited throughout are the landscapes that have shaped my poetic mind, understanding and, appreciation of the natural world.

PHOTO CREDITS

COVER and Hiking and Humming in Acadia - Wikimedia Commons, Acadia Scenic Coastal Road (commons.wikimedia.org/wiki/File:Acadia_Scenic_Coastal_Road_Aug_2017.jp)

Farmer Roscoe (The Philosopher) - painting by Ivan Olinsky, reprinted with permission.

Silence of the Backyard Sanctuary - photo by Kevin Geyson.

Hiking the Rugged Shore - Wikimedia Commons, Acadia National Park photo by Nadya Peek, Creative Commons.

Finding the Gingko Tree - Wikimedia Commons, Gingko by Famartin

Marginal Way, Ogunquit - Wikimedia Commons, Marginal Way, Captain-tucker, reprinted with permission (https://commons.m.wikimedia.org/wiki/User:Captain-tucker)

The Spirit Bear of Canada - photo by Jon Rawlinson.

Sea Shepherds - Narwals, NOAA Photolib Library, Public Domain.

Japanese Honeysuckle - Wikimedia Commons, Krzysztof Ziarnek, Kenraiz

Leap from Grace - Frog by Jen Payne, reprinted with permission.

Trees in the Winter Forest - Gemma Mathewson

CAROL LEAVITT ALTIERI

Carol Leavitt Altieri is retired from teaching English and American literature in New Haven Public Schools. She has published five books of poetry and won the Connecticut Environmental Award for helping to save the Griswold Airport Property. She loves hiking, reading and the whole world of nature.

Her previous poetry books include *In Beijing, There Are No Redwoods*; *The Isinglass River*; *The Jade Bower*; *Chronicles of Humans with Nature*; *Still Brooding on a Strong Branch*; *Parables of Passages*.